TABLE OF CONTENTS

Core Expectations.. 1

For Peace Corps Volunteers 1

Peace Corps/South Africa 2

History and Programs 2

    History of the Peace Corps in South Africa..................................... 2

    History and Future of Peace Corps Programming in South Africa 2

Country Overview: South Africa at a Glance 5

    History.. 5

    Government... 6

    Economy 7

    People and Culture 7

    Environment 8

Resources for Further Information 9

    General Information About South Africa 9

    Connect With Returned Volunteers and Other Invitees.................10

    Online Articles/Current News Sites About South Africa................10

    International Development Sites About South Africa 10

    Recommended Books 11

    Books About the History of the Peace Corps.................................11

    Books on the Volunteer Experience...12

Living Conditions and Volunteer Lifestyle...14

    Communications 14

    Mail 14

    Telephones 14

    Computer, Internet, and Email Access 15

    Housing and Site Location..15

    Living Allowance and Money Management 16

    Food and Diet..16

    Transportation 16

    Geography and Climate 17

Social Activities 17

Professionalism, Dress, and Behavior 18

Personal Safety 18

Rewards and Frustrations 19

Peace Corps Training 22

Pre-Service Training 22

Technical Training 22

Language Training 22

Cross-Cultural Training 23

Health Training 23

Safety Training 23

Additional Trainings During Volunteer Service 24

Your Health Care and Safety in South Africa 26

Health Issues in South Africa 26

Helping You Stay Healthy 26

Maintaining Your Health 27

Women's Health Information 28

Your Peace Corps Medical Kit 28

Medical Kit Contents 28

Before You Leave: A Medical Checklist 29

Safety and Security: Our Partnership 32

Factors that Contribute to Volunteer Risk 32

Staying Safe: Don't Be a Target for Crime 34

Support from Staff 35

Crime Data for South Africa 35

Volunteer Safety Support in South Africa 35

Diversity and Cross-Cultural Issues 38

Overview of Diversity in South Africa 38

What Might a Volunteer Face? 39

Possible Issues for Female Volunteers 39

Possible Issues for Volunteers of Color 39

Possible Issues for Senior Volunteers 39

Possible Issues for Gay, Lesbian, or Bisexual Volunteers...40

Possible Religious Issues for Volunteers 40

Possible Issues for Volunteers With Disabilities...40

Frequently Asked Questions...43

How much luggage am I allowed to bring to South Africa? 43

What is the electric current in South Africa? 43

How much money should I bring?..43

When can I take vacation and have people visit me?...43

Will my belongings be covered by insurance?..44

Do I need an international driver's license? 44

What should I bring as gifts for South Africa friends and my host family? 44

Where will my site assignment be when I finish training and how isolated will I be? ..44

How can my family contact me in an emergency? 44

Can I call home from South Africa? 45

Should I bring a cellular phone with me? 45

Will there be email and Internet access? Should I bring my computer?........................45

Welcome Letters from Country Volunteers 47

Packing List...50

Pre-Departure Checklist 53

Family..53

Passport/Travel 53

Medical/Health 53

Insurance 53

Personal Papers..53

Voting..54

Personal Effects 54

Financial Management 54

Contacting Peace Corps Headquarters 55

COUNTRY OVERVIEW: SOUTH AFRICA AT A GLANCE

History

The history of South Africa is marked by successive invasions by various groups, from the earliest hominids to the Khoisan and Bantu peoples to Portuguese explorers to Dutch and British colonists. These were followed by centuries of struggle for land and economic and political power.

The Portuguese were the first Europeans to reach the Cape of Good Hope, arriving in 1488. However, permanent white settlement did not begin until 1652, when the Dutch East India Company established a provisioning station in the Cape. In subsequent decades, French Huguenot refugees, the Dutch, and Germans began to settle in the Cape. Collectively, they form the Afrikaner segment of South Africa's current population. The establishment of these settlements had far reaching social and political effects on the groups already living in the area, leading to upheaval in their societies and subjugation of the people.

After British colonists seized the Cape of Good Hope in 1806, many of the Dutch who had settled there (the Boers) moved north in search of land and freedom from British rule. A mass migration, which came to be known as the Great Trek, began in the 1830s, when the British banned slavery and asserted equality of the races. In Afrikaner lore, the trek carried a strong biblical connection, in which the Voortrekkers (Afrikaans for "pioneers") were seeking not only independence but a promised land. Their violent encounters with Zulus in Natal added to the trek's epic drama and provided a foundation for Afrikaner nationalism. A turning point in the Zulu wars came on December 16, 1838, when the Boers killed 3,000 Zulus in a battle at "Blood" River. Initially called "Dingaan's Day," the event was celebrated nationally as the "Day of the Vow" until 1994, when it began being called the "Day of Reconciliation."

In the first Anglo-Boer war (1880-1881), known to Afrikaners as the War of Independence, the Boers quickly defeated British forces and established the Zuid Afrikaansche Republiek (ZAR). During a second Anglo-Boer war in 1899, the Boers' hatred of the British intensified as thousands of women and children were herded into concentration camps. After 26,000 Boers, mostly children, died in the camps, ZAR leaders reluctantly signed the Peace of Vereeniging in 1902, and the Boer republics became British colonies.

For the 80 percent African majority, little changed under British rule. Although nonwhites were promised freedom from "Boer slavery," the peace treaty did nothing to ensure their political rights, except in the Cape, where voting privileges were retained for whites, "Coloureds" (those of mixed race), and selected blacks. Political awareness grew, however, as Mohandas Gandhi began to work with Indian leaders in the colonies of Natal and Transvaal and African-led political groups started to develop.

In 1910, after seven years of negotiations, the four British colonies—Cape, Natal, Transvaal, and Orange Free State—were able to form the Union of South Africa, a dominion of the British empire with a parliamentary form of government.

The foundations of modern apartheid (which means "apartness") were laid not long after the union was established as a barrage of repressive legislation was passed. This legislation outlawed strikes by African workers, reserved skilled jobs for whites, banned Africans from military service, and tightened the pass laws that restricted movement by nonwhites.

Both the Afrikaner-based National Party (NP) and the South African Native Congress, which later became the African National Congress (ANC), were formed in 1912. The ANC's goals were the elimination of restrictions based on color and the enfranchisement of and parliamentary representation for blacks. Despite the party's efforts, the government continued to pass laws limiting the rights and freedoms of blacks.

In 1948, the NP ran and won on the platform of apartheid and began passing legislation that would codify and enforce an even stricter policy of racial separation and white domination. Through creative gerrymandering and other means, the NP managed to retain power for the next 46 years.

In the early 1960s, following a protest in Sharpeville in which 69 protesters were killed by police and 180 injured, the ANC and the Pan African Congress (PAC) were banned. Nelson Mandela and many other anti-apartheid leaders were convicted and imprisoned on charges of treason. The Sharpeville Massacre, as it became known, sparked international outrage, and appeals for economic sanctions and military and sporting boycotts against South Africa began in earnest worldwide.

Popular uprisings in black townships in 1976 and 1985 helped convince some NP members of the need for change. In February 1990, President F.W. de Klerk announced the unbanning of the ANC, the PAC, and all other anti-apartheid groups. Two weeks later, Nelson Mandela was released from prison. In 1991, many of the apartheid laws were abolished. A long series of negotiations ensued, resulting in the promulgation of a new constitution in December 1991. The country's first nonracially restricted elections, held April 26-29, 1994, resulted in the installation of Nelson Mandela as president on May 10, 1994. Thabo Mbeki was elected by Parliament to a second five-year term in April 2004 following the landslide general election victory of his ruling ANC. Mr. Mbeki took over as president when Nelson Mandela stepped down in mid-1999, but he is considered to have ruled the country almost since the ANC became South Africa's first democratically elected government in April 1994.

Government

South Africa is an independent republic with three branches of government. The executive branch houses the president (chief of state), who is elected to a five-year term by the

National Assembly. The legislative branch is a bicameral parliament consisting of 490 members in two chambers: the National Assembly (400 members), elected by a system of proportional representation, and the National Council of Provinces, consisting of 90 voting delegates (10 from each province) and 10 nonvoting delegates representing local government. The judicial branch includes the Constitution Court, which interprets and decides constitutional issues, and the Supreme Court of Appeal, which is the highest court for interpreting and deciding non-constitutional matters.

Economy

South Africa has a productive and industrialized economy that paradoxically exhibits many characteristics associated with developing countries, including a division of labor between formal and informal sectors and uneven distribution of wealth and income. The formal sector, based on mining, manufacturing, electronic commerce, services, and agriculture, is well-developed. The transition to a democratic government that began in the early 1990s stimulated a debate on economic polices to achieve sustained economic growth while simultaneously redressing the socioeconomic disparities created by apartheid. The initial blueprint to address this problem was the Reconstruction and Development Program, which was designed to improve the standard of living for the majority of the population by providing housing, basic services, education, and healthcare. Despite the nation's abundant wealth, 50 percent of the population was living below the national poverty line in 2000, and 26 percent was unemployed as of 2002, according to the CIA's World Factbook. In addition, the World Bank estimates that 13 percent of males and 14 percent of females ages 15 and older are functionally illiterate.

People and Culture

Until 1991, South African law divided the population into four major racial categories: Africans (blacks), whites, Coloureds, and Asians. Although this law has been abolished, many South Africans still view themselves and one another according to these categories. Africans constitute 77 percent of the population and consist of a number of ethnic groups (Ndebeles, Shangaans, Sothos, Swazis, Tswanas, Vendas, Xhosas, and Zulus). Whites, primarily descendants of Dutch, French, English, and German settlers, constitute 11 percent. Coloureds, people of mixed race primarily descending from the earliest settlers and the indigenous peoples, make up 9 percent of the population. Asians descending from Indian workers brought to South Africa in the mid-19th century to work on the sugar estates constitute 3 percent. To accommodate its diverse population, South Africa has 11 official languages: English, Afrikaans, Ndebele, Pedi, Sotho, Swazi, Tsonga, Tswana, Venda, Xhosa, and Zulu.

South Africa is predominantly a Christian country, but also has sizable Hindu, Muslim, and Jewish populations. Along with the major organized religions, animist beliefs are still strong in many areas of the country.

South Africa is truly a "rainbow nation." Although the tremendous wealth inherent in such diversity was not generally recognized within the country in the past, diversity is one of the national treasures of this society in transition.

Environment

South Africa lies north of 35 degrees south latitude, at the southernmost part of the African continent, and is surrounded on three sides by the Indian and Atlantic oceans. Bigger than California and Texas combined, the country's landscapes are as varied as they are dramatic: spectacular rocky coastlines and bone-dry deserts; miles of lush vineyards and orchards and barren, ghostly remains of gold and diamond mines; modern, industrial cities with affluent suburbs and small, remote villages that could be found anywhere in rural Africa.

Most of the land rests on a vast, saucer-shaped plateau that is 3,000 to 6,500 feet above sea level and bounded by the Great Escarpment. Framing this plateau is a narrow coastal strip. South Africa essentially is divided into three major parts: the huge interior plateau, called the Highveld; the Kalahari Basin, which borders Namibia and Botswana in the north; and the narrow coastal plain, called the Lowveld.

Only about 15 percent of the country is arable. Nevertheless, South Africa not only is self-sufficient in nearly all its food requirements, but it exports many crops, including fresh fruits and vegetables, cane sugar, and wine. Sheep and cattle are widely raised. Frozen rock lobsters, fish meal, and other products of the sea are also major exports.

Much of South Africa's wealth, however, comes not from what it has grown or raised above the ground but from what exists below. The discovery of diamonds at the DeBeers farm in Kimberley in 1871 and of the gold reef at Witwatersrand in 1886 changed South Africa forever from an agricultural nation to the continent's economic and industrial giant. As of 2001, the country possessed and mined 73 percent of the world's chrome reserves, 56 percent of its platinum group metals, 46 percent of its gold, 44 percent of its vanadium, and 80 percent of its manganese. Other reserves include nickel, copper, zinc, bituminous coal, and gem-quality and industrial diamonds.

Perhaps South Africa's most valuable and enduring natural resource is its rich and varied wildlife. The country is home to Africa's largest land mammal (the African elephant), as well as its second and third biggest (the white rhinoceros and the hippopotamus, respectively), its tallest (the giraffe), its fastest (the cheetah), and its smallest (the pygmy shrew). You are more likely to see Africa's "Big Five"—lion, leopard, elephant, buffalo, and black rhino—in one of South Africa's 10 major nature reserves than anywhere else on the continent. A tremendous variety of reptiles and more than 900 species of birds also inhabit the country.

RESOURCES FOR FURTHER INFORMATION

Following is a list of websites for additional information about the Peace Corps, South Africa, and to connect you to returned Volunteers and other invitees. Please keep in mind that although we try to make sure all these links are active and current, we cannot guarantee it. If you do not have access to the Internet, visit your local library. Libraries offer free Internet usage and often let you print information to take home.

A note of caution: As you surf the Internet, be aware that you may find bulletin boards and chat rooms in which people are free to express opinions about the Peace Corps based on their own experience, including comments by those who were unhappy with their choice to serve in the Peace Corps. These opinions are not those of the Peace Corps or the U.S. government, and we hope you will keep in mind that no two people experience their service in the same way.

General Information About South Africa

www.countrywatch.com

On this site, you can learn anything from what time it is in the capital of South Africa to how to convert from the dollar to the South Africa currency. Just click on South Africa and go from there.

www.lonelyplanet.com/destinations

Visit this site for general travel advice about almost any country in the world.

www.state.gov

The State Department's website issues background notes periodically about countries around the world. Find South Africa and learn more about its social and political history. You can also go to the site's international travel section to check on conditions that may affect your safety.

www.psr.keele.ac.uk/official.htm

This includes links to all the official sites for governments worldwide.

www.geography.about.com/library/maps/blindex.htm

This online world atlas includes maps and geographical information, and each country page contains links to other sites, such as the Library of Congress, that contain comprehensive historical, social, and political background.

www.cyberschoolbus.un.org/infonation/info.asp

This United Nations site allows you to search for statistical information for member states of the U.N.

www.worldinformation.com

This site provides an additional source of current and historical information about countries around the world.

Connect With Returned Volunteers and Other Invitees

www.rpcv.org

This is the site of the National Peace Corps Association, made up of returned Volunteers. On this site you can find links to all the Web pages of the "Friends of" groups for most countries of service, comprised of former Volunteers who served in those countries. There are also regional groups that frequently get together for social events and local volunteer activities.

www.PeaceCorpsWorldwide.org

This site is hosted by a group of returned Volunteer writers. It is a monthly online publication of essays and Volunteer accounts of their Peace Corps service.

Online Articles/Current News Sites About South Africa

http://www.mg.co.za/

Site of the Mail and Guardian, a progressive weekly newspaper

www.iol.co.za

Site of the Sunday Independent, which features articles on development issues

http://www.idasa.org.za/index.asp

Institute for a Democratic Alternative in South Africa

http://www.csvr.org.za/

Centre for the Study of Violence and Reconciliation

International Development Sites About South Africa

www.unaids.org

A United Nations site with thorough information on the AIDS epidemic

www.usaid.gov

U.S. Agency for International Development

www.worldbank.org

World Bank, for information related to development aid

www.cdcnpin.org/

The Centers for Disease Control and Prevention's National Prevention Information Network, for information on HIV/AIDS worldwide

www.sahealthinfo.org

Health knowledge network for southern Africa; includes up to-date information on HIV/AIDS in South Africa

Recommended Books

- Frederickson, George M. *White Supremacy: A Comparative Study of American and South African History.* London: Oxford University Press, 1981. Discusses the origins and nature of white racism in both contexts.

- Kuzwayo, Ellen. *Call Me Woman.* London: Picador Africa, 2004.

- Mandela, Nelson. *Long Walk to Freedom: Autobiography of Nelson Mandela.* London: Little, Brown, 1995.

- Paton, Alan. *Cry, the Beloved Country.* New York: Charles Scribner's, 1995. Classic South African tale of murder and the breakdown of family and civil society.

- Sparks, Allister. *Beyond the Miracle: Inside the New South Africa.* Chicago; IL: University of Chicago Press, 2004.

- Stober, Paul and Barbara Ludman (eds.) *Mail and Guardian A-Z of South African Politics.*

Books About the History of the Peace Corps

- Hoffman, Elizabeth Cobbs. *All You Need is Love: The Peace Corps and the Spirit of the 1960s.* Cambridge, Mass.: Harvard University Press, 2000.

- Rice, Gerald T. *The Bold Experiment: JFK's Peace Corps.* Notre Dame, Ind.: University of Notre Dame Press, 1985.

- Stossel, Scott. *Sarge: The Life and Times of Sargent Shriver.* Washington, D.C.: Smithsonian Institution Press, 2004.

- Meisler, Stanley. *When the World Calls: The Inside Story of the Peace Corps and its First 50 Years*. Boston, Mass.: Beacon Press, 2011.

Books on the Volunteer Experience

- Dirlam, Sharon. *Beyond Siberia: Two Years in a Forgotten Place*. Santa Barbara, Calif.: McSeas Books, 2004.

- Casebolt, Marjorie DeMoss. *Margarita: A Guatemalan Peace Corps Experience*. Gig Harbor, Wash.: Red Apple Publishing, 2000.

- Erdman, Sarah. Nine Hills to Nambonkaha: Two Years in the Heart of an African Village. New York, N.Y.: Picador, 2003.

- Hessler, Peter. *River Town: Two Years on the Yangtze*. New York, N.Y.: Perennial, 2001.

- Kennedy, Geraldine ed. *From the Center of the Earth: Stories out of the Peace Corps*. Santa Monica, Calif.: Clover Park Press, 1991.

- Thompsen, Moritz. *Living Poor: A Peace Corps Chronicle*. Seattle, Wash.: University of Washington Press, 1997 (reprint).

LIVING CONDITIONS AND VOLUNTEER LIFESTYLE

Communications
Mail

Few countries in the world offer the level of mail service we consider normal in the United States. If you come here expecting U.S. standards, you will be in for a lot of frustration. Mail takes a minimum of two to three weeks to arrive, often longer. Some mail may simply not arrive (this is rare, but it does happen). Although we do not want to sound too discouraging, communication can become a very sensitive issue when one is thousands of miles from family and friends. We think it is best to forewarn you about mail service in this part of the world. Advise your family and friends to number their letters and to write "Airmail" on the envelopes.

Packages sent via airmail can take from six to nine weeks; those sent by surface mail take around six months. If someone is sending you a package, a suggestion is to keep it small and use a padded envelope so it will be treated like a letter.

Despite the potential delays, we strongly encourage you to write to your family regularly and to number your letters. Family members typically become worried when they do not hear from you, so advise them that mail is sporadic and that they should not worry if they do not receive your letters regularly. Volunteers in South Africa do not receive duty-free privileges, so be aware that you may be charged duty on items you mail to yourself before you arrive. Volunteers normally receive mail at the Peace Corps office during training, but obtain a local post office box once assigned to their sites.

Packages received at the Peace Corps/South Africa office will be delivered to you only when staff is traveling in your area. Letters will be forwarded to you once a month.

Your address during training will be:

> Your Name
> Peace Corps
> PO Box 9536
> Pretoria 0001
> South Africa

Telephones

Upon arrival in South Africa, every trainee is given an opportunity to e-mail and telephone a family member or friend in the U.S. However, during most of pre-service training, you will have infrequent opportunities to use telephones or Internet, if at all. This is because we want you to become thoroughly immersed in living and learning about your community and host family.

International phone service to South Africa is good, though expensive. AT&T, MCI, and other U.S. companies provide direct long-distance service to the United States. Using a calling card is cheaper than calling collect.

Cell phones are widely available in South Africa. You will find that most people have cell phones, even in the remotest parts of the country. A cell phone purchased in the United States may not work here, and many Volunteers choose to purchase their own cell phones here.

The Peace Corps office in South Africa can be reached by direct dialing from the United States. The number is 011.27.12.344.4255. The fax number is 011.27.12.343.7774.

Volunteers are not permitted to use the telephones at the office to call family and friends unless the call pertains to an emergency and is approved in advance by the country director.

Computer, Internet, and Email Access

Computers are available in South Africa, but most Volunteers in rural areas will find few, if any computers. Your site may not have electricity, so the ability to use a personal computer is not guaranteed. More and more Volunteers find that their school or organization has a computer, but knowledge of how to use the computer is limited. The Peace Corps office in Pretoria has computers available in the Volunteer resource center for Volunteer use. (Peace Corps staff computers are not available for Volunteer use.) Volunteers normally use these computers for committee work and to complete service documents. We encourage Volunteers to use computers that may be available at district/circuit offices and sponsoring agencies for any grant or proposal writing to ensure that counterparts participate in the proposal-writing process. In most large cities and towns, Volunteers are able to access email at Internet cafes. Volunteers' monthly living allowance includes money to cover use of Internet cafes.

Housing and Site Location

All Volunteers live with a host family at a site located anywhere from one hour to nine hours from Pretoria, the capital. Proximity to another Volunteer varies from site to site.

Your host agency will provide safe and adequate housing—in accordance with the Peace Corps' site selection criteria—that is likely to consist of a private room inside a family's house or a room in an outside building within a family compound. Housing varies from mud houses with either thatch or tin roofs to brick homes with tin roofs. You need to be very flexible in your housing expectations because there is no guarantee that you will have running water or electricity. If you do not, you will collect your water from a well or borehole and spend your evenings reading by candlelight or lantern.

The sponsoring agency or host family will provide you with basic items (e.g., a bed, mattress, desk/table, straight chair, and cupboard for hanging clothing or storage). Each Volunteer will receive an allowance in local currency to purchase needed settling-in items, as well as a water filter provided by the Peace Corps.

Living Allowance and Money Management

As a Volunteer, you will receive a modest living allowance, paid in rand, that will allow you to live on a par with your colleagues and co-workers. The amount of this allowance is based on regular surveys of Volunteers and the cost of living in South Africa. The living allowance is paid quarterly into Volunteer bank accounts, so the ability to manage funds wisely is important. The allowance is intended to cover the cost of food, utilities, household supplies, clothing, recreation and entertainment, transportation, reading materials, and other incidentals. You will also receive a leave allowance of $24 per month (standard in all Peace Corps countries) for the upcoming three months, paid in local currency, along with your living allowance each quarter.

Most credit cards and ATM cards are widely accepted in South Africa. Current Volunteers suggest that you bring cash and credit cards for vacation travel. The amount of cash depends on the amount of traveling you plan to do while serving in South Africa.

Food and Diet

The staple food in communities where Volunteers live and work is maize (corn), prepared as a thick porridge called pap and eaten with vegetables or a sauce. Many fresh fruits and vegetables are available in South Africa, and with a little creativity, you can enjoy a varied diet even in rural areas. Volunteers either prepare their own food or share meals with their host family. You can determine what the best arrangement is for you once you have been assigned a site. Fruits and vegetables are available seasonally, which means some things will not be in the market year-round. A variety of meat and dairy products are also available. Though most South Africans are meat-eaters, vegetarians are able to eat well here after becoming familiar with local food items and their preparation. Most South Africans do not understand vegetarianism and will not normally be prepared to serve a vegetarian meal if you are a guest in their home. However, a sensitive explanation of your preferences will be accepted. Most vegetarian Volunteers have no difficulty after an initial adjustment period.

Transportation

Volunteers' primary modes of transportation in South Africa are public buses and combies (minivans) loaded with people and goods. Combies travel between towns on irregular schedules (i.e., when full), so travel on this form of transport is never a timed affair. Bus schedules are fairly regular, but buses generally are not available in some rural areas.

Many Volunteers receive an all-terrain bicycle (along with a helmet) to facilitate their work. It is Peace Corps' policy that helmets be worn when riding. Note that these bikes are men's bikes, which can be difficult for women to ride when wearing a skirt. Many female Volunteers wear shorts under their skirt to solve this problem.

Volunteers are not allowed to drive, own, or operate motor vehicles, including motorcycles (two- or three-wheeled). Violation of this policy can result in your being terminated from Volunteer service.

Geography and Climate

Most world maps give a poor idea of how large South Africa actually is. At 472,276 square miles, it is five times the size of the United Kingdom and one-eighth the size of the United States. Kruger National Park alone is as big as Wales, and the distance from Johannesburg to Cape Town is the same as that from London to Rome. The country's 1,835 miles of coastline border the Atlantic and Indian oceans, which meet at Cape Agulhas, the southernmost tip of Africa.

South Africa is south of the equator, so its seasons will be the opposite of what you are accustomed to. January is midsummer and July is midwinter. Johannesburg, Pretoria, and the rest of the eastern Highveld have a dry, sunny climate, with maximum winter temperatures of about 70 degrees Fahrenheit, and crisp nights, with temperatures dropping to around 40 degrees. Between October and April, the daytime temperature can rise into the 80s, with frequent late-afternoon thunderstorms. Temperatures can get hotter in the Great Karroo, the semi desert heart of the three Cape provinces; in the Kalahari region; and in the Lowveld of the Eastern and Northern Transvaal. The terrain ranges in altitude from sea level to South Africa's highest peak, Injasuti (11,178 feet), in the Drakensberg, near the border with Lesotho, and contains ecosystems from tropical forest to desert dunes. Almost every known crop can be grown somewhere in the country.

Social Activities

Your social life will vary depending on where you are located, but is likely to include taking part in various community festivities and celebrations. The most common form of entertainment is socializing with friends and neighbors. There are four television stations, which broadcast both South African and American productions, and several radio stations that play popular music. In communities with electricity, watching TV is a major pastime.

Some Volunteers visit other Volunteers on weekends and during holidays. However, we encourage Volunteers to remain at their sites in order to develop relationships in their community and promote the second goal of the Peace Corps, cultural exchange. Most regional towns have movies, Internet cafes, and restaurants that Volunteers can take advantage of when in town for shopping or other business.

Professionalism, Dress, and Behavior

South Africans place an importance on professional dress in the workplace. Dress is more conservative in rural areas than it is in the major cities. In the United States, we often view clothes as a reflection of our individuality. In South Africa, your clothes are seen as a sign of your respect for those around you. South Africans do not appreciate clothes that are dirty, have holes in them, or are too revealing. Wearing them will reduce the amount of respect given to you and therefore your effectiveness. While jeans and T-shirts are acceptable as casual wear, it is more common to see men in shirts with collars and casual slacks and women in casual dresses, skirts, or slacks with blouses or shirts. South Africans generally do not hesitate to voice their opinions when they consider someone's dress to be embarrassing or inappropriate.

The Peace Corps is still a young organization in South Africa, and as a Volunteer you will be expected to behave in a way that fosters respect within your community and reflects well on both the Peace Corps and the United States. Your dress, behavior, and attitude will all contribute to how well the agency is received. You will have the status of an invited guest, and thus you will have to be sensitive to the habits, tastes, and taboos of your hosts. If you have reservations about your ability or willingness to do so, you should reevaluate your decision to become a Peace Corps Volunteer. Volunteering to work effectively in another culture requires a level of sacrifice and flexibility that can be difficult for some people. Behavior that jeopardizes the Peace Corps program or your personal safety in South Africa cannot be tolerated and may lead to administrative separation—a decision by the Peace Corps to terminate your service.

Personal Safety

More detailed information about the Peace Corps' approach to safety is contained in the "Health Care and Safety" chapter, but it is an important issue and cannot be overemphasized. As stated in the Volunteer Handbook, becoming a Peace Corps Volunteer entails certain safety risks. Living and traveling in an unfamiliar environment (oftentimes alone), having a limited understanding of local language and culture, and being perceived as well-off are some of the factors that can put a Volunteer at risk. Many Volunteers experience varying degrees of unwanted attention and harassment. Petty thefts and burglaries are not uncommon, and incidents of physical and sexual assault do occur, although most South Africa Volunteers complete their two years of service without incident. The Peace Corps has established procedures and policies designed to help you reduce your risks and enhance your safety and security. These procedures and policies, in addition to safety training, will be provided once you arrive in South Africa. Using these tools, you are expected to take responsibility for your safety and well-being.

Each staff member at the Peace Corps is committed to providing Volunteers with the support they need to successfully meet the challenges they will face to have a safe, healthy, and productive service. We encourage Volunteers and families to look at our safety and security information on the Peace Corps website at **www.peacecorps.gov/safety**.

Information on these pages gives messages on Volunteer health and Volunteer safety. There is a section titled "Safety and Security – Our Partnership." Among topics addressed are the risks of serving as a Volunteer, posts' safety support systems, and emergency planning and communications.

The AIDS pandemic strikes across all social strata in many Peace Corps countries. The loss of teachers has crippled education systems, while illness and disability drains family income and forces governments and donors to redirect limited resources from other priorities. The fear and uncertainty AIDS causes has led to increased domestic violence and stigmatizing of people living with HIV/AIDS, isolating them from friends and family and cutting them off from economic opportunities. As a Peace Corps Volunteer, you will confront these issues on a very personal level. It is important to be aware of the high emotional toll that disease, death, and violence can have on Volunteers. As you strive to integrate into your community, you will develop relationships with local people who might die during your service. Because of the AIDS pandemic, some Volunteers will be regularly meeting with HIV-positive people and working with training staff, office staff, and host family members living with AIDS. Volunteers need to prepare themselves to embrace these relationships in a sensitive and positive manner. Likewise, malaria and malnutrition, motor vehicle accidents and other unintentional injuries, domestic violence and corporal punishment are problems a Volunteer may confront. You will need to anticipate these situations and utilize supportive resources available throughout your training and service to maintain your own emotional strength so that you can continue to be of service to your community.

Rewards and Frustrations

Although the potential for job satisfaction is quite high, like all Volunteers, you will encounter numerous frustrations. Perceptions of time that are very different from those in the United States, financial or other challenges of collaborating agencies, lack of expected support in a timely manner, and being perceived as very rich can be challenging. Peace Corps Volunteers often describe their experience of adapting to a new culture and environment as an intense series of emotional peaks and valleys. You will be given a great deal of responsibility and independence in your work—perhaps more than in any other job you ever have. Often you will need to motivate yourself and others with little to no guidance. You might work for months with little visible impact and without receiving feedback on your work. Development is a slow process. You must possess the self-confidence, patience, and vision to continue working toward long-term goals without seeing immediate results.

To deal with these difficulties you will need maturity, flexibility, open-mindedness, compassion, and resourcefulness. Judging by the experience of former Volunteers, the peaks are well worth the difficult times, and most Volunteers leave South Africa feeling that they gained more than they sacrificed during their service. If you are able to make the commitment to integrate into your community, work hard, and revel in small accomplishments, you will have a truly life altering experience.

PEACE CORPS TRAINING

Pre-Service Training

Training is an essential and ongoing part of your Peace Corps service. Pre-service training will give you enough skills and information to begin your adjustment to and service in South Africa. It is the first "reality test" of your life as a Volunteer, which will help you make an informed commitment when you swear in as a Peace Corps Volunteer.

The 8- to 10-week pre-service training in South Africa is community based, meaning that the bulk of the training takes place in a community similar to where you will be placed as a Volunteer. The training staff will design a learning environment with experiences and meetings designed to allow you to develop the knowledge and skills needed for your work as a Volunteer. There will be sessions on language, community integration, cross-cultural communication, development issues, health and personal safety, and technical skills appropriate to your assignment. Throughout your training, you will live with a South African family and work in villages and schools.

At the onset of training, the training staff will outline the training goals and assessment criteria that each trainee has to reach before becoming a Volunteer. Evaluation of your performance during training will be based on a continual dialogue between you and the training staff. The training manager, along with other training staff, will work with you to achieve the training goals by providing you feedback throughout training.

Technical Training

Technical training will prepare you to work in South Africa by building on the skills you already have and helping you develop new skills in a manner appropriate to the needs of the country. The Peace Corps staff, South Africa experts, and current Volunteers will conduct the training program. Training places great emphasis on learning how to transfer the skills you have to the community in which you will serve as a Volunteer.

Technical training will include sessions on the general economic and political environment in South Africa and strategies for working within such a framework. You will review your technical sector's goals and will meet with the South Africa agencies and organizations that invited the Peace Corps to assist them. You will be supported and evaluated throughout the training to build the confidence and skills you need to undertake your project activities and be a productive member of your community.

Language Training

As a Peace Corps Volunteer, you will find that language skills are key to personal and professional satisfaction during your service. These skills are critical to your job performance, they help you integrate into your community, and they can ease your personal adaptation to the new surroundings. Therefore, language training is at the heart of the training program. You must successfully meet minimum language requirements to complete training and become a Volunteer. South Africa language instructors teach formal language classes five days a week in small groups of four to five people.

Your language training will incorporate a community-based approach. In addition to classroom time, you will be given assignments to work on outside of the classroom and with your host family. The goal is to get you to a point of basic social communication skills so you can practice and develop language skills further once you are at your site. Prior to being sworn in as a Volunteer, you will work on strategies to continue language studies during your service.

Cross-Cultural Training

As part of your pre-service training, you will live with a South Africa host family. This experience is designed to ease your transition to life at your site. Families go through an orientation conducted by Peace Corps staff to explain the purpose of pre-service training and to assist them in helping you adapt to living in South Africa. Many Volunteers form strong and lasting friendships with their host families.

Cross-cultural and community development training will help you improve your communication skills and understand your role as a facilitator of development. You will be exposed to topics such as community mobilization, conflict resolution, gender and development, nonformal and adult education strategies, and political structures.

Health Training

During pre-service training, you will be given basic medical training and information. You will be expected to practice preventive health care and to take responsibility for your own health by adhering to all medical policies. Trainees are required to attend all medical sessions. The topics include preventive health measures and minor and major medical issues that you might encounter while in South Africa. Nutrition, mental health, setting up a safe living compound, and how to avoid HIV/AIDS and other sexually transmitted diseases (STDs) are also covered.

Safety Training

During the safety training sessions, you will learn how to adopt a lifestyle that reduces your risks at home, at work, and during your travels. You will also learn appropriate, effective strategies for coping with unwanted attention and about your individual responsibility for promoting safety throughout your service.

Additional Trainings During Volunteer Service

In its commitment to institutionalize quality training, the Peace Corps has implemented a training system that provides Volunteers with continual opportunities to examine their commitment to Peace Corps service while increasing their technical and cross-cultural skills. During service, there are usually three training events. The titles and objectives for those trainings are as follows:

- In-service training: Provides an opportunity for Volunteers to upgrade their technical, language, and project development skills while sharing their experiences and reaffirming their commitment after having served for three to six months.

- Midterm conference (done in conjunction with technical sector in-service): Assists Volunteers in reviewing their first year, reassessing their personal and project objectives, and planning for their second year of service.

- Close-of-service conference: Prepares Volunteers for the future after Peace Corps service and reviews their respective projects and personal experiences.

The number, length, and design of these trainings are adapted to country-specific needs and conditions. The key to the training system is that training events are integrated and interrelated, from the pre-departure orientation through the end of your service, and are planned, implemented, and evaluated cooperatively by the training staff, Peace Corps staff, and Volunteers.

YOUR HEALTH CARE AND
SAFETY IN SOUTH AFRICA

The Peace Corps' highest priority is maintaining the good health and safety of every Volunteer. Peace Corps medical programs emphasize the preventive, rather than the curative, approach to disease. The Peace Corps in South Africa maintains a clinic with a full-time medical officer, who takes care of Volunteers' primary health care needs. Additional medical services, such as testing and basic treatment, are also available in South Africa at local hospitals. If you become seriously ill, you will be transported either to an American-standard medical facility in the region or to the United States.

Health Issues in South Africa

Major health problems among Peace Corps Volunteers in South Africa are rare and are often the result of a Volunteer's not taking preventive measure to stay healthy. The most common health problems here are minor ones also found in the United States, such as colds, diarrhea, skin infections, headaches, sinus infections, dental problems, minor injuries, STDs, adjustment disorders, and emotional problems. These problems may be compounded by living in another culture.

The most common health concerns here are HIV/AIDS, gastrointestinal infections, alcoholism, and skin disorders. Because malaria is endemic in parts of South Africa, you may be required to take antimalarial pills. You will also be vaccinated against hepatitis A and B, meningitis, tetanus, typhoid, and rabies.

Monitoring mental health conditions is difficult at best. There are Alcoholics Anonymous facilities in the larger cities, but there are no support groups in rural areas. Alcohol is an integral part of many social interactions in South Africa, and you may be pressured to drink even if you choose not to, as there is little understanding of alcoholism. Long-term counseling is not offered to Volunteers. Short-term therapy (i.e., maximum of three sessions) may be offered if you have a specific issue.

Helping You Stay Healthy

The Peace Corps will provide you with all the necessary inoculations, medications, and information to stay healthy. Upon your arrival in South Africa, you will receive a medical handbook. At the end of training, you will receive a medical kit with supplies to take care of mild illnesses and first aid needs. The contents of the kit are listed later in this chapter.

During pre-service training, you will have access to basic medical supplies through the medical officer. However, you will be responsible for your own supply of prescription drugs and any other specific medical supplies you require, as the Peace Corps will not order these items during training. Please bring a three-month supply of any prescription drugs you use, since they may not be available here and it may take several months for shipments to arrive.

You will have physicals at midservice and at the end of your service. If you develop a serious medical problem during your service, the medical officer in South Africa will consult with the Office of Medical Services in Washington, D.C. If it is determined that your condition cannot be treated in South Africa, you may be sent out of the country for further evaluation and care.

Maintaining Your Health

As a Volunteer, you must accept considerable responsibility for your own health. Proper precautions will significantly reduce your risk of serious illness or injury. The adage "An ounce of prevention ..." becomes extremely important in areas where diagnostic and treatment facilities are not up to the standards of the United States. The most important of your responsibilities in South Africa is to take the following preventive measures:

Malaria is hyperendemic and present in some of the areas where Volunteers serve. It can kill you if left untreated, so prophylaxis against malaria is mandatory for Volunteers serving in these areas, and early recognition of infection is extremely important. Other preventive measures, such as the use of Peace Corps-issued mosquito nets, insect repellents, and screens on windows and doors, are strongly encouraged.

Rabies is prevalent throughout the country, so you will receive a series of immunizations against it during your training period. If you are exposed to an animal that is known or suspected to have rabies, you must inform the medical officer at once so that you can receive post-exposure booster shots. Many illnesses that afflict Volunteers worldwide are entirely preventable if proper food and water precautions are taken. These illnesses include food poisoning, parasitic infections, hepatitis A, dysentery, Guinea worms, tapeworms, and typhoid fever. Your medical officer will discuss specific standards for water and food preparation in South Africa during pre-service training.

Abstinence is the only certain choice for preventing infection with HIV and other sexually transmitted diseases. You are taking risks if you choose to be sexually active. To lessen risk, use a condom every time you have sex. Whether your partner is a host country citizen, a fellow Volunteer, or anyone else, do not assume this person is free of HIV/AIDS or other STDs. You will receive more information from the medical officer about this important issue.

Volunteers are expected to adhere to an effective means of birth control to prevent an unplanned pregnancy. Your medical officer can help you decide on the most appropriate method to suit your individual needs. Contraceptive methods are available without charge from the medical officer.

It is critical to your health that you promptly report to the medical office or other designated facility for scheduled immunizations, and that you let the medical officer know immediately of significant illnesses and injuries.

Women's Health Information

Pregnancy is treated in the same manner as other Volunteer health conditions that require medical attention but also have programmatic ramifications. The Peace Corps is responsible for determining the medical risk and the availability of appropriate medical care if the Volunteer remains in-country. Given the circumstances under which Volunteers live and work in Peace Corps countries, it is rare that the Peace Corps' medical and programmatic standards for continued service during pregnancy can be met.

If feminine hygiene products are not available for you to purchase on the local market, the Peace Corps medical officer in South Africa will provide them. If you require a specific product, please bring a three-month supply with you.

Your Peace Corps Medical Kit

The Peace Corps medical officer will provide you with a kit that contains basic items necessary to prevent and treat illnesses that may occur during service. Kit items can be periodically restocked at the medical office.

Medical Kit Contents

Ace bandages
Adhesive tape
American Red Cross First Aid & Safety
   Handbook
Antacid tablets (Tums)
Antibiotic ointment (Bacitracin/Neomycin/
   Polymycin B)
Antiseptic antimicrobial skin cleaner
   (Hibiclens)
Band-Aids
Butterfly closures
Calamine lotion
Cepacol lozenges
Condoms

Dental floss
Diphenhydramine HCL 25 mg (Benadryl)
Insect repellent stick (Cutter's)
Iodine tablets (for water purification)
Lip balm (Chapstick)
Oral rehydration salts
Oral thermometer (Fahrenheit)
Pseudoephedrine HCL 30 mg (Sudafed)
Robitussin-DM lozenges (for cough)
Scissors
Sterile gauze pads
Tetrahydrozaline eyedrops (Visine)
Tinactin (antifungal cream)
Tweezers

Before You Leave: A Medical Checklist

If there has been any change in your health – physical, mental, or dental – since you submitted your examination reports to the Peace Corps, you must immediately notify the Office of Medical Services. Failure to disclose new illnesses, injuries, allergies, or pregnancy can endanger your health and may jeopardize your eligibility to serve.

If your dental exam was done more than a year ago, or if your physical exam is more than two years old, contact the Office of Medical Services to find out whether you need to update your records. If your dentist or Peace Corps dental consultant has recommended that you undergo dental treatment or repair, you must complete that work and make sure your dentist sends requested confirmation reports or X-rays to the Office of Medical Services.

If you wish to avoid having duplicate vaccinations, contact your physician's office to obtain a copy of your immunization record and bring it to your pre-departure orientation. If you have any immunizations prior to Peace Corps service, the Peace Corps cannot reimburse you for the cost. The Peace Corps will provide all the immunizations necessary for your overseas assignment, either at your pre-departure orientation or shortly after you arrive in South Africa. You do not need to begin taking malaria medication prior to departure.

Bring a three-month supply of any prescription or over-the-counter medication you use on a regular basis, including birth control pills. Although the Peace Corps cannot reimburse you for this three-month supply, it will order refills during your service. While awaiting shipment – which can take several months – you will be dependent on your own medication supply. The Peace Corps will not pay for herbal or nonprescribed medications, such as St. John's wort, glucosamine, selenium, or antioxidant supplements.

You are encouraged to bring copies of medical prescriptions signed by your physician. This is not a requirement, but they might come in handy if you are questioned in transit about carrying a three-month supply of prescription drugs.

If you wear eyeglasses, bring two pairs with you – a pair and a spare. If a pair breaks, the Peace Corps will replace them, using the information your doctor in the United States provided on the eyeglasses form during your examination. The Peace Corps discourages you from using contact lenses during your service to reduce your risk of developing a serious infection or other eye disease. Most Peace Corps countries do not have appropriate water and sanitation to support eye care with the use of contact lenses. The Peace Corps will not supply or replace contact lenses or associated solutions unless an ophthalmologist has recommended their use for a specific medical condition and the Peace Corps' Office of Medical Services has given approval.

If you are eligible for Medicare, are over 50 years of age, or have a health condition that may restrict your future participation in health care plans, you may wish to consult an insurance specialist about unique coverage needs before your departure. The Peace Corps will provide all necessary health care from the time you leave for your pre-departure orientation until you complete your service. When you finish, you will be entitled to the post-service health care benefits described in the Peace Corps Volunteer Handbook. You may wish to consider keeping an existing health plan in effect during your service if you think age or pre-existing conditions might prevent you from re-enrolling in your current plan when you return home.

SAFETY AND SECURITY: OUR PARTNERSHIP

Serving as a Volunteer overseas entails certain safety and security risks. Living and traveling in an unfamiliar environment, a limited understanding of the local language and culture, and the perception of being a wealthy American are some of the factors that can put a Volunteer at risk. Property theft and burglaries are not uncommon. Incidents of physical and sexual assault do occur, although almost all Volunteers complete their two years of service without serious personal safety problems.

Beyond knowing that Peace Corps approaches safety and security as a partnership with you, it might be helpful to see how this partnership works. Peace Corps has policies, procedures, and training in place to promote your safety. We depend on you to follow those policies and to put into practice what you have learned. An example of how this works in practice – in this case to help manage the risk of burglary – is:

- Peace Corps assesses the security environment where you will live and work
- Peace Corps inspects the house where you will live according to established security criteria
- Peace Corps provides you with resources to take measures such as installing new locks
- Peace Corps ensures you are welcomed by host country authorities in your new community
- Peace Corps responds to security concerns that you raise
- You lock your doors and windows
- You adopt a lifestyle appropriate to the community where you live
- You get to know neighbors
- You decide if purchasing personal articles insurance is appropriate for you
- You don't change residences before being authorized by Peace Corps
- You communicate concerns that you have to Peace Corps staff

Factors that Contribute to Volunteer Risk

There are several factors that can heighten a Volunteer's risk, many of which are within the Volunteer's control. By far the most common crime that Volunteers experience is theft. Thefts often occur when Volunteers are away from their sites, in crowded locations (such as markets or on public transportation), and when leaving items unattended.

Before you depart for South Africa there are several measures you can take to reduce your risk:

- Leave valuable objects in the U.S.
- Leave copies of important documents and account numbers with someone you trust in the U.S.
- Purchase a hidden money pouch or "dummy" wallet as a decoy
- Purchase personal articles insurance

After you arrive in South Africa, you will receive more detailed information about common crimes, factors that contribute to Volunteer risk, and local strategies to reduce that risk. For example, Volunteers in South Africa learn to:

- Choose safe routes and times for travel, and travel with someone trusted by the community whenever possible
- Make sure one's personal appearance is respectful of local customs
- Avoid high-crime areas
- Know the local language to get help in an emergency
- Make friends with local people who are respected in the community
- Limit alcohol consumption

As you can see from this list, you must be willing to work hard and adapt your lifestyle to minimize the potential for being a target for crime. As with anywhere in the world, crime does exist in South Africa. You can reduce your risk by avoiding situations that place you at risk and by taking precautions. Crime at the village or town level is less frequent than in the large cities; people know each other and generally are less likely to steal from their neighbors. Tourist attractions in large towns are favorite worksites for pickpockets.

The following are other security concerns in South Africa of which you should be aware:

Motor vehicle accidents. Speed, unsafe vehicles, alcohol, and road rage contribute to most traffic fatalities. Volunteers are strongly encouraged to wear seat belts when available. Using public buses and minibuses is difficult to avoid, and they tend to be overcrowded. Vehicles are often not up to Western safety standards, and driving under the influence is not uncommon. Traveling after dark is highly discouraged.

Robbery/burglary. The homes of some Volunteers have been robbed in the past, but most robberies, muggings, and thefts have occurred in towns and large cities. Therefore, it is important to exercise caution at all times. The Peace Corps requires host families to install burglar bars and locks in all Volunteers' homes. We will advise you on proper home safety during training.

Harassment. Volunteers have reported varying levels of harassment over money, age, gender, racial or ethnic background, religious beliefs, and sex or sexual orientation. This can happen anywhere—at work, at one's site, in towns, or while traveling on public transportation. Strategies for dealing and coping with harassment are discussed extensively during training.

Alcohol abuse. South Africa has a higher rate of alcoholism than the United States does, and Volunteers have reported being approached by intoxicated people asking for money, sex, and/or alcohol. It is best to avoid bars and other places that sell alcohol, particularly at night. Volunteers must act responsibly with regard to their own alcohol consumption to preserve their reputation and working relationships in the community.

Sexual assault. Volunteers in South Africa have been targets of sexual assault. Cross-cultural differences in gender relations and alcohol consumption are often associated with sexual assaults. Sexual assault will be addressed in pre-service training. Volunteers are strongly urged to report all assaults or threats of assault to the Peace Corps medical officer or other staff so that they can respond with appropriate support.

Note that sex outside of marriage is not looked upon favorably in South Africa and may jeopardize your safety or your ability to develop mutually respectful relationships in your community and at your job. South Africans often hold Volunteers to a different standard of sexual morality than they hold themselves to. Also note that promiscuity puts both men and women at risk for STDs, particularly HIV/AIDS.

Gay, lesbian, and bisexual Volunteers will have to practice discretion. Some South Africans are homophobic, and there have been instances of violence toward individuals who are presumed to be or who are openly gay. The Peace Corps is committed to providing support for all Volunteers regardless of sexual orientation.

While whistles and exclamations may be fairly common on the street, this behavior can be reduced if you dress conservatively, abide by local cultural norms, and respond according to the training you will receive.

Staying Safe: Don't Be a Target for Crime

You must be prepared to take on a large degree of responsibility for your own safety. You can make yourself less of a target, ensure that your home is secure, and develop relationships in your community that will make you an unlikely victim of crime. While the factors that contribute to your risk in South Africa may be different, in many ways you can do what you would do if you moved to a new city anywhere: Be cautious, check things out, ask questions, learn about your neighborhood, know where the more risky locations are, use common sense, and be aware. You can reduce your vulnerability to crime by integrating into your community, learning the local language, acting responsibly, and abiding by Peace

Corps policies and procedures. Serving safely and effectively in South Africa will require that you accept some restrictions on your current lifestyle.

Support from Staff

If a trainee or Volunteer is the victim of a safety incident, Peace Corps staff is prepared to provide support. All Peace Corps posts have procedures in place to respond to incidents of crime committed against Volunteers. The first priority for all posts in the aftermath of an incident is to ensure the Volunteer is safe and receiving medical treatment as needed. After assuring the safety of the Volunteer, Peace Corps staff response may include reassessing the Volunteer's worksite and housing arrangements and making any adjustments, as needed. In some cases, the nature of the incident may necessitate a site or housing transfer. Peace Corps staff will also assist Volunteers with preserving their rights to pursue legal sanctions against the perpetrators of the crime. It is very important that Volunteers report incidents as they occur, not only to protect their peer Volunteers, but also to preserve the future right to prosecute. Should Volunteers decide later in the process that they want to proceed with the prosecution of their assailant, this option may no longer exist if the evidence of the event has not been preserved at the time of the incident.

Crime Data for South Africa

Crime data and statistics for South Africa, which is updated yearly, are available at the following link: **http://www.peacecorps.gov/countrydata/southafrica**. Please take the time to review this important information.

Few Peace Corps Volunteers are victims of serious crimes and crimes that do occur overseas are investigated and prosecuted by local authorities through the local courts system. If you are the victim of a crime, you will decide if you wish to pursue prosecution. If you decide to prosecute, Peace Corps will be there to assist you. One of our tasks is to ensure you are fully informed of your options and understand how the local legal process works. Peace Corps will help you ensure your rights are protected to the fullest extent possible under the laws of the country.

If you are the victim of a serious crime, you will learn how to get to a safe location as quickly as possible and contact your Peace Corps office. It's important that you notify Peace Corps as soon as you can so Peace Corps can provide you with the help you need.

Volunteer Safety Support in South Africa

The Peace Corps' approach to safety is a five-pronged plan to help you stay safe during your service and includes the following: information sharing, Volunteer training, site selection criteria, a detailed emergency action plan, and protocols for addressing safety and security incidents. South Africa's in-country safety program is outlined below.

Delete information and insert text here if your country's safety approach differs from the following, but each country's safety plan should closely resemble what follows.

The Peace Corps/South Africa office will keep you informed of any issues that may impact Volunteer safety through **information sharing**. Regular updates will be provided in Volunteer newsletters and in memorandums from the country director. In the event of a critical situation or emergency, you will be contacted through the emergency communication network. An important component of the capacity of Peace Corps to keep you informed is your buy-in to the partnership concept with the Peace Corps staff. It is expected that you will do your part in ensuring that Peace Corps staff members are kept apprised of your movements in-country so they are able to inform you.

Volunteer training will include sessions on specific safety and security issues in South Africa. This training will prepare you to adopt a culturally appropriate lifestyle and exercise judgment that promotes safety and reduces risk in your home, at work, and while traveling. Safety training is offered throughout service and is integrated into the language, cross-cultural aspects, health, and other components of training. You will be expected to successfully complete all training competencies in a variety of areas, including safety and security, as a condition of service.

Certain **site selection criteria** are used to determine safe housing for Volunteers before their arrival. The Peace Corps staff works closely with host communities and counterpart agencies to help prepare them for a Volunteer's arrival and to establish expectations of their respective roles in supporting the Volunteer. Each site is inspected before the Volunteer's arrival to ensure placement in appropriate, safe, and secure housing and worksites. Site selection is based, in part, on any relevant site history; access to medical, banking, postal, and other essential services; availability of communications, transportation, and markets; different housing options and living arrangements; and other Volunteer support needs.

You will also learn about Peace Corps/South Africa's **detailed emergency action plan**, which is implemented in the event of civil or political unrest or a natural disaster. When you arrive at your site, you will complete and submit a site locator form with your address, contact information, and a map to your house. If there is a security threat, you will gather with other Volunteers in South Africa at predetermined locations until the situation is resolved or the Peace Corps decides to evacuate.

Finally, in order for the Peace Corps to be fully responsive to the needs of Volunteers, it is imperative that Volunteers immediately report any security incident to the Peace Corps office. The Peace Corps has established protocols for **addressing safety and security incidents** in a timely and appropriate manner, and it collects and evaluates safety and security data to track trends and develop strategies to minimize risks to future Volunteers.

DIVERSITY AND CROSS-CULTURAL ISSUES

In fulfilling its mandate to share the face of America with host countries, the Peace Corps is making special efforts to assure that all of America's richness is reflected in the Volunteer corps. More Americans of color are serving in today's Peace Corps than at any time in recent history. Differences in race, ethnic background, age, religion, and sexual orientation are expected and welcomed among our Volunteers. Part of the Peace Corps' mission is to help dispel any notion that Americans are all of one origin or race and to establish that each of us is as thoroughly American as the other despite our many differences.

Our diversity helps us accomplish that goal. In other ways, however, it poses challenges. In South Africa, as in other Peace Corps host countries, Volunteers' behavior, lifestyle, background, and beliefs are judged in a cultural context very different from their own. Certain personal perspectives or characteristics commonly accepted in the United States may be quite uncommon, unacceptable, or even repressed in South Africa.

Outside of South Africa's capital, residents of rural communities have had relatively little direct exposure to other cultures, races, religions, and lifestyles. What people view as typical American behavior or norms may be a misconception, such as the belief that all Americans are rich and have blond hair and blue eyes. The people of South Africa are justly known for their generous hospitality to foreigners; however, members of the community in which you will live may display a range of reactions to cultural differences that you present.

To ease the transition and adapt to life in South Africa, you may need to make some temporary, yet fundamental compromises in how you present yourself as an American and as an individual. For example, female trainees and Volunteers may not be able to exercise the independence available to them in the United States; political discussions need to be handled with great care; and some of your personal beliefs may best remain undisclosed. You will need to develop techniques and personal strategies for coping with these and other limitations. The Peace Corps staff will lead diversity and sensitivity discussions during pre-service training and will be on call to provide support, but the challenge ultimately will be your own.

Overview of Diversity in South Africa

The Peace Corps staff in South Africa recognizes the adjustment issues that come with diversity and will endeavor to provide support and guidance. During pre-service training, several sessions will be held to discuss diversity and coping mechanisms. We look forward to having male and female Volunteers from a variety of races, ethnic groups, ages, religions, and sexual orientations, and hope that you will become part of a diverse group of Americans who take pride in supporting one another and demonstrating the richness of American culture.

What Might a Volunteer Face?

Possible Issues for Female Volunteers

South Africa has a patriarchal culture. This may not seem to be the case when one considers the number of women in high-level government and private-sector positions. However, men and women are expected to fulfill distinct roles and responsibilities. In rural areas female Volunteers may find extremely conservative attitudes regarding gender equality. Likewise, the behavior of female Volunteers is more often scrutinized or criticized than that of their male peers. Although the Peace Corps emphasizes understanding of and sensitivity toward other cultures, it will occasionally be necessary to explain or defend why you believe something or behave a certain way. Female Volunteers may find that they are constantly asked about their marital status and whether they have children because women are expected to be married.

Possible Issues for Volunteers of Color

South Africa is still divided along color lines as a result of the legacy of apartheid. All Volunteers, regardless of their color, will receive certain privileges or face discrimination because of the color of their skin. Volunteers will find themselves placed in one of four categories: white, Coloured, black, or Asian. This labeling has been a major source of frustration for Volunteers, and developing strategies for handling this frustration is a task in and of itself. Peace Corps/South Africa Volunteers have developed a diversity committee to explore the diversity of both South Africa and the United States and have established forums for discussions and exchanges.

At one time or another, all Volunteers serving in South Africa may find that services are denied or offered based on skin color; that white skin brings privileges that may not be wanted or deserved; that they constantly have to explain that they are an American and not a South African white, Coloured, Asian, or black; that skin color determines the level of trust or confidence people have in their ability; that they are accepted more readily into the culture than other Volunteers because of skin color; that they are engaged in conversations with South Africans who hold adamant views against another group; that services are offered to them but denied to another Volunteer or counterpart who is accompanying them; that they are the subject of disparaging remarks based on current or historical roles of certain ethnic groups (e.g., assuming Asians are merchants); and that people hold stereotyped views based on behavior observed in American films and sitcoms (e.g., most African Americans are "gang-bangers").

Possible Issues for Senior Volunteers

Respect comes with age in South Africa. Younger Volunteers may have to work harder than their older colleagues to be accepted as professionals. Senior Volunteers are seen as those with the most wisdom and experience and other valuable things to offer. South Africans are often surprised by the amount of energy and the physical fitness of senior Volunteers.

South Africans may also be curious about senior female Volunteers, puzzled as to why they seem to have no spouse or children even if they have the pictures to prove otherwise.

Possible Issues for Gay, Lesbian, or Bisexual Volunteers

Gay, lesbian, and bisexual Volunteers must know that South Africa is a very conservative society. Many South Africans, especially in rural areas, are in denial that homosexuality exists in their culture. Thus any display of your sexuality will be severely frowned upon. Some previous Volunteers have decided to serve their time in South Africa under the cloak of silence to prevent adverse effects on their relations with their community and co-workers. You can find some helpful information at www.geocities.com/lgbrpcv/, a website affiliated with the National Peace Corps Association that provides information on serving in the Peace Corps as a gay or lesbian.

A recommended resource for support and advice prior to and during your service is the Lesbian, Gay, Bisexual & Transgender U.S. Peace Corps Alumni website at **www.lgbrpcv.org**.

Possible Religious Issues for Volunteers

Religion is a very important part of the lives of people in rural areas. There are a variety of groups and denominations and you will be asked more than once to attend someone's church. On any Sunday, whether in rural areas or cities, you can distinguish among the various groups by their distinctive uniforms. Volunteers not in the practice of attending church may be challenged to explain their reluctance, but it is possible to decline to attend if the church or religious practice is not of one's own denomination. In addition, prayer is an important part of any function. No meeting, event, or even the beginning of school can start without a prayer, and people may be insulted if they do. This may take getting used to, but Volunteers have found effective ways to cope with these challenges and have come to feel quite at home in South Africa.

Possible Issues for Volunteers With Disabilities

As part of the medical clearance process, the Peace Corps Office of Medical Services determined that you were physically and emotionally capable, with or without reasonable accommodations, to perform a full tour of Volunteer service in South Africa without unreasonable risk of harm to yourself or interruption of service. The Peace Corps/ South Africa staff will work with disabled Volunteers to make reasonable accommodations for them in training, housing, jobsites, or other areas to enable them to serve safely and effectively.

There is little infrastructure in the country to accommodate individuals with physical disabilities. No schools or other facilities in rural areas teach disabled children or accommodate people with disabilities. Peace Corps/South Africa staff will work with disabled Volunteers to make reasonable accommodations for them in training, housing, job sites, or other areas to enable them to serve safely and effectively. As part of the medical clearance process, the Peace Corps Office of Medical Services determined that you were physically and emotionally capable, with or without reasonable accommodations, to perform a full tour of service in South Africa without unreasonable risk of harm to yourself or interruption of service.

FREQUENTLY ASKED QUESTIONS

This list has been compiled by Volunteers serving in South Africa and is based on their experience. Use it as an informal guide in making your own list, bearing in mind that each experience is individual. There is no perfect list! You obviously cannot bring everything on the list, so consider those items that make the most sense to you personally and professionally. You can always have things sent to you later. As you decide what to bring, keep in mind that you have a 100-pound weight limit on baggage. And remember, you can get almost everything you need in South Africa.

How much luggage am I allowed to bring to South Africa?

Most airlines have baggage size and weight limits and assess charges for transport of baggage that exceeds those limits. The Peace Corps has its own size and weight limits and will not pay the cost of transport for baggage that exceeds these limits. The Peace Corps' allowance is two checked pieces of luggage with combined dimensions of both pieces not to exceed 107 inches (length + width + height) and a carry-on bag with dimensions of no more than 45 inches. Checked baggage should not exceed 100 pounds total with a maximum weight of 50 pounds for any one bag.

Peace Corps Volunteers are not allowed to take pets, weapons, explosives, radio transmitters (shortwave radios are permitted), automobiles, or motorcycles to their overseas assignments. Do not pack flammable materials or liquids such as lighter fluid, cleaning solvents, hair spray, or aerosol containers. This is an important safety precaution.

What is the electric current in South Africa?

If you have working electricity, the current is 50 cycles, 220 volts. There may be surges and brownouts, which put a strain on appliances. The Peace Corps does not provide transformers. We recommend tape players that use D batteries because C batteries are a little harder to find in rural areas. AA and watch and calculator batteries are easy to find.

How much money should I bring?

Volunteers are expected to live at the same level as the people in their community. You will be given a settling-in allowance and a monthly living allowance, which should cover your expenses. Volunteers often wish to bring additional money for vacation travel to other countries. Credit cards and traveler's checks are preferable to cash. If you choose to bring extra money, bring the amount that will suit your own travel plans and needs.

When can I take vacation and have people visit me?

Each Volunteer accrues two vacation days per month of service (excluding training). Leave may not be taken during training, the first three months of service, or the last three months of service, except in conjunction with an authorized emergency leave. Family and friends are welcome to visit you after pre-service training and the first three months of service as long as their stay does not interfere with your work. Extended stays at your site are not encouraged and may require permission from your country director. The Peace Corps is not able to provide your visitors with visa, medical, or travel assistance.

Will my belongings be covered by insurance?

The Peace Corps does not provide insurance coverage for personal effects; Volunteers are ultimately responsible for the safekeeping of their personal belongings. However, you can purchase personal property insurance before you leave. If you wish, you may contact your own insurance company; additionally, insurance application forms will be provided, and we encourage you to consider them carefully. Volunteers should not ship or take valuable items overseas. Jewelry, watches, radios, cameras, and expensive appliances are subject to loss, theft, and breakage, and in many places, satisfactory maintenance and repair services are not available.

Do I need an international driver's license?

Volunteers in South Africa do not need an international driver's license because they are prohibited from operating privately owned motorized vehicles. Most urban travel is by bus or taxi. Rural travel ranges from buses and minibuses to trucks, bicycles, and lots of walking. On very rare occasions, a Volunteer may be asked to drive a sponsor's vehicle, but this can occur only with prior written permission from the country director. Should this occur, the Volunteer may obtain a local driver's license. A U.S. driver's license will facilitate the process, so bring it with you just in case.

What should I bring as gifts for South Africa friends and my host family?

This is not a requirement. A token of friendship is sufficient. Some gift suggestions include knickknacks for the house; pictures, books, or calendars of American scenes; souvenirs from your area; hard candies that will not melt or spoil; or photos to give away.

Where will my site assignment be when I finish training and how isolated will I be?

Peace Corps trainees are not assigned to individual sites until after they have completed pre-service training. This gives Peace Corps staff the opportunity to assess each trainee's technical and language skills prior to assigning sites, in addition to finalizing site selections with their ministry counterparts. If feasible, you may have the opportunity to provide input on your site preferences, including geographical location, distance from other Volunteers, and living conditions. However, keep in mind that many factors influence the site selection process and that the Peace Corps cannot guarantee placement where you would ideally like to be. Most Volunteers live in small towns or in rural villages and are usually within one hour from another Volunteer. Some sites require a 10- to 12-hour drive from the capital.

How can my family contact me in an emergency?

The Peace Corps' Office of Special Services (OSS) provides assistance in handling emergencies affecting trainees and Volunteers or their families. Before leaving the United States, instruct your family to notify the Office of Special Services immediately if an emergency arises, such as a serious illness or death of a family member. During normal business hours, the number for the Office of Special Services is 855.855.1961, then select option 2; or directly at 202-692-1470. After normal business hours and on weekends and holidays, the OSS duty officer can be reached at the above number. For non-emergency questions, your family can get information from your country desk staff at the Peace Corps by calling 855.855.1961.

Can I call home from South Africa?

International phone service to and from South Africa is very good. Calling cards such as those offered by AT&T, MCI, and Sprint can be used in-country. Some Volunteers purchase their own cell phones and receive calls from home instead calling home. Some host families may have telephones in their homes.

Should I bring a cellular phone with me?

No. The systems here are different from those used in the United States. South Africa has two cellular service providers, and the Peace Corps staff is equipped with cellphones to attend to emergency calls. Volunteers who have personal cellphones are not always able to get service from their village.

Will there be email and Internet access? Should I bring my computer?

Many businesses and individuals in the capital and in some larger cities have Internet access. There are Internet cafes or businesses offering Internet service in all major cities and most large towns. Volunteers may be limited to writing and receiving e-mail on their occasional visits to the capital or to regional towns. Before leaving the United States, many Volunteers sign up for free e-mail accounts, such as those offered by Yahoo!, Gmail, or Hotmail, which they can access worldwide. Some Volunteers have brought their laptop computers, though they are responsible for insuring and maintaining the computer. The Peace Corps will not replace stolen computers and strongly encourages those who bring them to get personal property insurance. Because of the high value of laptops, owners significantly increase their risk of becoming a victim of crime. Additionally, gaining Internet access via your laptop is probably a remote possibility because very few Volunteers have telephone lines in their homes or adequate lines in their community.

WELCOME LETTERS FROM COUNTRY VOLUNTEERS

South Africa is truly one of the most beautiful places on Earth. It's not only the physical beauty of the landscape but, rather, the integrity of the people that wins most Volunteers' hearts. Keep in mind that you are about to enter into communities that have absolutely no idea of who you are and your life before you arrived. However, South Africans will open up their homes and hearts while teaching you their culture and language. This will greatly influence your adaptation to your new home for the next two years.

—Rohan Jeremiah

Dare to perceive, understand their rich culture. To recognize, comprehend their subtle manner. Join in tasting their robust nature. Witness their genteel charm. Examine the profound beauty of their artful crafts. With insight, dare to tread their life path with insight Feel their spirit.

—Candy Plaza

My job as a Peace Corps Volunteer is to work with teachers in schools as well as to help with community development. When I finally took the Peace Corps oath and moved to my new village, I was stunned by the welcome I received from my schools and community members. Each school held a celebration in my honor with marching, singing, dancers, skits, and speeches. Present were the learners, teachers, parents, school governing board, traditional chiefs, and community members. My host father took a day off from work to attend my key school celebration. Wow, I began to worry, how am I going to live up to the appreciation of these wonderful people?

Slowly I've come to realize that I am truly appreciated. I don't think that the people expect miracles; they just want friendly guidance and a helping hand in their struggle to make a new country. It's a good feeling when a teacher tells me, "We teachers think you have really helped us a lot." Then, too, there are the beautiful smiles on the children's faces as they greet me with "Good morning" (regardless of the time of day) using their new English.

—Joyce Perry

Leave your preconceptions behind; allow South Africa to surprise and educate you, to strengthen those ideals that led you across the world to help, like nowhere else can. The true beauty of this place lies far beyond any of its scenery. It is in the air and is only visible to those searching for it. You might feel a flash of it in the smile of an old, old man with a handshake that lasts a whole conversation and a kind, fair, most dignified spirit that has withstood abuse, isolation, and hatred that may go forever unspoken and unwritten. Next to his smile and the strength of its forgiveness, its survival, the velvety mountains will shrink and seem a silly object of admiration.

At other times, the scenery will fade away completely when a prejudice so old and ugly thorny jumps out from some corner to snarl and foam at you. It will happen. You may find yourself counting on people seething with hatred and working with people destroyed by it. But please do not start to click your heels together and chant, "There is no place like home, there is no place like home ..." (It does not work; I have tried it.) Instead, open your eyes to the opportunity and fill your thoughts with the smile of that old man or whoever it is that shows you the strength of the human spirit while you are here. They will. It is your job to recognize and honor all that dignity.

—Anna Domenico

We have been through many frustrations of being misunderstood and being embarrassed by our lack of understanding the culture and language. We have been frustrated, and sometimes angered, by the conditions in the schools and by the attitudes of the teachers and school management. We have learned to dislike the combie rides and the effort it takes to get anywhere. We have often become irritated with the days and nights of sweating in the humid heat, and yearn for an air-conditioned home and car. But we have begun to see the humor in the miscommunications, and embarrassment has turned to acceptance of our place here. We have found that being angered by the conditions in the schools can be abated by trying to understand the cultural history and by having minor successes and huge epiphanies. We have accepted the combie experience as an opportunity to get to know the villagers and to experience the local mode of transport. We have even become accustomed to the heat, and have learned to appreciate a gentle breeze, a shade tree, and a cloudy day.

—Jay Atherton

I can remember sitting in America sifting through the Peace Corps package I was sent, looking for the answers to all my questions. What will I do? What will it feel like? How will my village see me? And I didn't understand why no one said, "Here, this is what you will feel."

Now I know why South Africa unfolds differently to each pair of eyes, to each set of listening ears. And yours are not mine, so what I know may not be what you learn. But what I can tell you is: Few things are as voracious as South African bugs, as stupid as South African sheep, as beautiful as the South African sunset, as refreshing as South

African gogos (grandmothers), as abused as South African donkeys, or as bewildering as a South African Peace Corps experience.

—Linnea Ashley

I can remember sitting in my small room thinking, "What can I possibly do here?" Just as the thought crossed my mind, my younger South African sister came to my room and said, "I can't tell you how happy I am to have you here; you've already taught me that I too, as a young girl, can leave home on my own and help others." That statement was my driving force throughout my two-year stay. My just being here made a difference.

—Emily Coonfield

PACKING LIST

This list has been compiled by Volunteers serving in South Africa and is based on their experience. Use it as an informal guide in making your own list, bearing in mind that each experience is individual. There is no perfect list! You obviously cannot bring everything on the list, so consider those items that make the most sense to you personally and professionally. You can always have things sent to you later. As you decide what to bring, keep in mind that you have an 100-pound weight limit on baggage. And remember, you can get almost everything you need in South Africa.

General Clothing

- Warm coat/jacket (not necessarily down; fleece works well and can be layered)
- Waterproof rain jacket/poncho
- Windbreaker
- Durable jeans (for weekends and travel)
- Two or three sweaters (lightweight cotton and wool)
- Two or three pairs of walking-length shorts
- Long thermal underwear
- Good socks, including thick ones
- Baseball cap or sun hat
- Swimsuit and sportswear
- Belts
- Exercise gear (shorts for women may or may not be appropriate, depending on your site)

For Men

Men dress neatly and professionally in all workplaces, which means dress slacks or nice khakis, dress shirts, and dress shoes/loafers. Schoolteachers in particular are expected to wear ties while on duty. Jeans are not allowed to be worn at work.

- Two or three dress slacks/khakis
- Plenty of cotton underwear
- Three or four cotton dress shirts (button-down, both long and short sleeve)
- Two or three polo shirts
- One sport coat or suit
- Two or three ties

- T-shirts (neutral colors)

For Women

Women dress in a stylish and professional manner in workplaces, which means dresses, skirts and blouses, and dress shoes (flat or low-heeled, with good support and rubber soles) or sandals. Short shorts, miniskirts, and tops that show a lot of skin (e.g., halter tops with spaghetti straps) are inappropriate for women in village settings.

- Three to five dresses or skirts (knee length or longer)
- Two to four lightweight polyester/cotton blouses (short or long sleeve)
- T-shirts (neutral colors)
- Tights to wear with skirts in winter
- Plenty of cotton underwear and bras
- Heavy-duty sports bra
- Cotton half slips (knee and ankle length)

Shoes

- Comfortable dress shoes or loafers for men
- Dress shoes with flat or low heels for women
- Athletic shoes
- Waterproof hiking boots
- Flip-flops/shower shoes

People who wear larger sizes (12+ for men, 10+ for women), wide sizes, or corrective shoes should consider bringing an extra pair or two of shoes, as such shoes are difficult to find here.

Personal Hygiene and Toiletry Items

All the little things you need to keep your life running smoothly are available locally at prices comparable to those in the United States, so do not burden yourself with them. But bring enough toiletries to get you through training, as you will be in a rural setting where supplies may be limited.

- Two pairs of contact lenses or prescription eyeglasses (sunglasses are a must, so bring an extra pair; the Peace Corps will not replace prescription sunglasses)
- Prescription drugs (bring a three-month supply to last until the Peace Corps can reorder them)

Kitchen

You can easily purchase any needed supplies (dishes, pots, glasses, utensils), so do not use your 80 pounds on these items. However, you might want to bring your favorite cookbook.

Miscellaneous

- Two towels (to have during training)
- Stationery and envelopes to last during the eight to 10 weeks of pre-service training
- Watch—durable, water-resistant, inexpensive
- Reliable alarm clock
- Money belt that fits under your clothes
- Small sewing kit
- Radio/cassette/CD player/iPod or other mp3 player
- Camera (35 mm point-and-shoot; film can be bought and developed here)
- Laptop with flash disk and plug adapter (optional)
- Small binoculars—handy for spotting birds/animals in the parks
- Swiss army knife or Leatherman
- Camping equipment if you like camping (e.g., sleeping bag, backpack, and small tent; also available locally)
- Solar-powered, rechargeable batteries with charger
- Water bottle (e.g., Nalgene)
- Pictures of hometown, historical sites, family, and friends
- U.S. stamps (letters can often be mailed by people traveling back home)
- Maps of the United States and the world (good as teaching aids and wall hangings)
- Small flashlight and extra bulbs
- Guidebooks on the region
- Paperback novels (to swap after reading)
- Journal
- Hobby materials like sketching pads and pencils
- Musical instruments
- Games (Scrabble, cards, chess, Frisbee, etc.)
- Work gloves (for gardeners)

PRE-DEPARTURE CHECKLIST

The following list consists of suggestions for you to consider as you prepare to live outside the United States for two years. Not all items will be relevant to everyone, and the list does not include everything you should make arrangements for.

Family

- Notify family that they can call the Peace Corps' Counseling and Outreach Unit at any time if there is a critical illness or death of a family member (24-hour telephone number: 1-855-855-1961, then press 2; or directly at 202-692-1470).

- Give the Peace Corps' On the Home Front handbook to family and friends.

Passport/Travel

- Forward to the Peace Corps travel office all paperwork for the Peace Corps passport and visas.

- Verify that your luggage meets the size and weight limits for international travel.

- Obtain a personal passport if you plan to travel after your service ends. (Your Peace Corps passport will expire three months after you finish your service, so if you plan to travel longer, you will need a regular passport.)

Medical/Health

- Complete any needed dental and medical work.

- If you wear glasses, bring two pairs.

- Arrange to bring a three-month supply of all medications (including birth control pills) you are currently taking.

Insurance

- Make arrangements to maintain life insurance coverage.

- Arrange to maintain supplemental health coverage while you are away. (Even though the Peace Corps is responsible for your health care during Peace Corps service overseas, it is advisable for people who have pre-existing conditions to arrange for the continuation of their supplemental health coverage. If there is a lapse in coverage, it is often difficult and expensive to be reinstated.)

- Arrange to continue Medicare coverage if applicable.

Personal Papers

- Bring a copy of your certificate of marriage or divorce.

Voting

- Register to vote in the state of your home of record. (Many state universities consider voting and payment of state taxes as evidence of residence in that state.)

- Obtain a voter registration card and take it with you overseas.

- Arrange to have an absentee ballot forwarded to you overseas.

Personal Effects

- Purchase personal property insurance to extend from the time you leave your home for service overseas until the time you complete your service and return to the United States.

Financial Management

- Keep a bank account in your name in the U.S.

- Obtain student loan deferment forms from the lender or loan service.

- Execute a Power of Attorney for the management of your property and business.

- Arrange for deductions from your readjustment allowance to pay alimony, child support, and other debts through the Office of Volunteer Financial Operations at 855.855.1961, extension 1770.

- Place all important papers—mortgages, deeds, stocks, and bonds—in a safe deposit box or with an attorney or other caretaker.

CONTACTING PEACE CORPS HEADQUARTERS

This list of numbers will help connect you with the appropriate office at Peace Corps headquarters to answer various questions. You can use the toll-free number and extension or dial directly using the local numbers provided. Be sure to leave the toll-free number and extensions with your family so they can contact you in the event of an emergency.

Peace Corps Headquarters Toll-free Number: 855.855.1961, Press 1 or ext. # (see below)

Peace Corps' Mailing Address: Peace Corps Headquarters
1111 20th Street, NW
Washington, DC 20526

Questions About:	Staff:	Toll-Free Ext:	Direct/Local #:
Responding to an Invitation	Office of Placement	x1840	202.692.1840
Country Information	Greg Pachuta Desk Officer / (South Africa & Swaziland) southafrica@peacecorps.gov	X2197	202.692.2197
Plane Tickets, Passports, Visas, or other travel matters:	CWT SATO Travel	x1170	202.692.1170
Legal Clearance	Office of Placement	x1840	202.692.1840
Medical Clearance & Forms Processing (includes dental)	Screening Nurse	x1500	202.692.1500
Medical Reimbursements (handled by a subcontractor)	Seven Corners	N/A	202.692.1538 800.335.0611
Loan Deferments, Taxes, Financial Operations	Office Of Volunteer and PSC Financial Services	x1770	202.692.1770
Readjustment Allowance Withdrawals, Power of Attorney, Staging (Pre-Departure Orientation), and Reporting Instructions	Office of Staging *Note: You will receive comprehensive information (hotel and flight arrangements) three to five weeks prior to departure. This information is not available sooner.*	x1865	202.692.1865
Family Emergencies (to get information to a Volunteer overseas) 24 hours	Office of Special Services	x1470	202.692.1470